WEIRD WORK

by Ben Hubbard
Illustrated by El Primo Ramón

Contents

A World of Work 2
Sleeping on the Job 4
Life in a Line 6
Window Washing Wonders 8
Water Workers 10
Seeking a Sense of Smell 12
Best Pet Food Flavour 14
Dangerous Divers 16
The Most Boring Job? 18
Bicycle Fishing 20
The World's Weirdest Jobs? 22
Glossary and Index 24

OXFORD
UNIVERSITY PRESS

A World of Work

What would you like to do when you grow up?
Here are some jobs you may have heard of already:

firefighter

author

farmer

footballer

computer game designer

astronaut

There are also lots of exciting jobs that you have probably never heard of. It might not have occurred to you that people can work outside a skyscraper, or in a queue, or at the bottom of a pond. Some people even work right next to other people's armpits!

This book is all about the weirdest jobs in the world — and the weirdest places to do them.

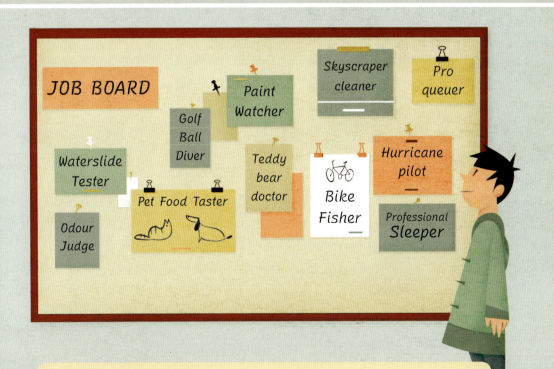

If something occurs to you, you think of it. Has it ever occurred to you that someone could work on the outside of a skyscraper?

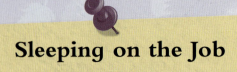

Sleeping on the Job

Have you heard the saying 'sleeping on the job'? This means you are not concentrating on your work. However, what if your job is to sleep?

Some hotels pay people to test their beds. They want to make sure an uncomfortable bed does not ruin a guest's stay. The testers have to write a report about the bed and the hotel room.

testing the comfort of hotel pillows

Can you think of another word for 'ruin'?

Being a **professional** sleeper may sound easy, but apparently it can be tricky. Some professional sleepers work in research centres, helping scientists to learn more about sleep. They are asked to lie on the same bed for several nights in a row – even if it is uncomfortable. Sometimes they are attached to wires to measure how they are sleeping.

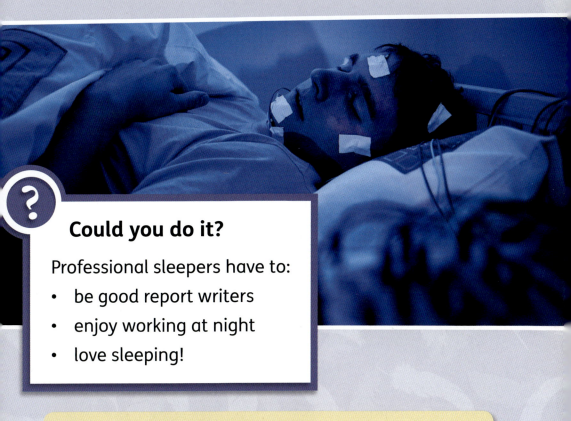

Could you do it?

Professional sleepers have to:
- be good report writers
- enjoy working at night
- love sleeping!

If you use 'apparently' in a sentence, are you sure about what has happened, or are you guessing based on what you have seen or heard?

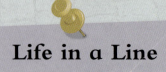

Life in a Line

People often have to stand in a queue. Queues for exciting or special events can last for days and stretch for miles. Some people even bring tents so they can sleep overnight in the queue.

people queuing for a sports event

Queuing can be boring and take up lots of time. What if someone else could do your queuing for you? Professional queuers stand in line for people. When the queuer reaches the front of the line they swap places with the person who hired them.

people queuing in bad weather

Could you do it?

Professional queuers have to:
- enjoy both cold and hot weather
- not mind getting bored
- be patient!

Window Washing Wonders

The world's tallest buildings are thousands of metres high and often covered with windows. These windows get dirty. So how are they cleaned?

You need a big team of skyscraper window cleaners! They work high above the ground, on the outside of the building. They are tied on with ropes to keep them safe.

Window cleaners need <u>steady</u> hands so they don't drop things.

Can you hold this book so that it is <u>steady</u>? Can you hold it so that it is unsteady?

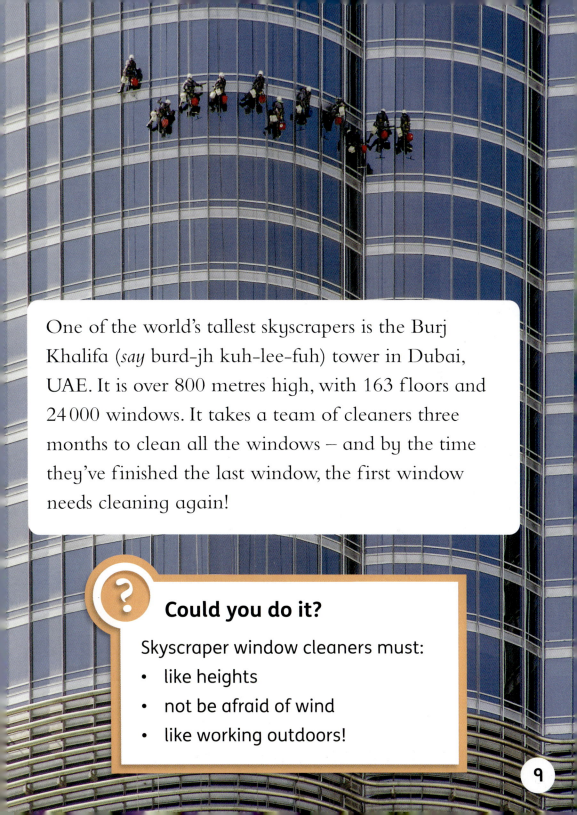

One of the world's tallest skyscrapers is the Burj Khalifa (*say* burd-jh kuh-lee-fuh) tower in Dubai, UAE. It is over 800 metres high, with 163 floors and 24 000 windows. It takes a team of cleaners three months to clean all the windows – and by the time they've finished the last window, the first window needs cleaning again!

Could you do it?

Skyscraper window cleaners must:
- like heights
- not be afraid of wind
- like working outdoors!

Water Workers

Have you ever been to a water park? These are fun parks with swimming pools, wave pools and water slides. Water is pumped down water slides to give you a <u>swift</u> ride to the bottom. Some slides are over 400 metres long and very steep.

Did you know?

One of the world's tallest water slides is in Brazil. The slide is taller than eleven giraffes standing on top of one another!

Can you move <u>swiftly</u> across the room?

A water slide tester must check the safety of each slide before anyone else is allowed on it. They fly around the world testing water slides to make sure they are safe, and have a big splash and **thrill** factor.

Being a water slide tester sounds fun, but the testers have to ride the slides even in cold weather. Brrr!

Could you do it?

Water slide testers have to:
- love water
- be happy to travel
- like steep slides!

Seeking a Sense of Smell

Asking people to sniff bad smells may seem <u>cruel</u>, but some people do it for a job. They are called **odour** judges.

People who make **deodorant** hire odour judges to check that the deodorant works. The odour judges have to sniff people's armpits after they have used the deodorant.

Can you explain why it might seem <u>cruel</u> or mean to make people sniff bad smells?

Other odour judges work for people that make paper towels. They have to check that the paper towels never smell bad, even after they have been used to clean up a mess.

Odour judges also work for food companies, to make sure the food smells good.

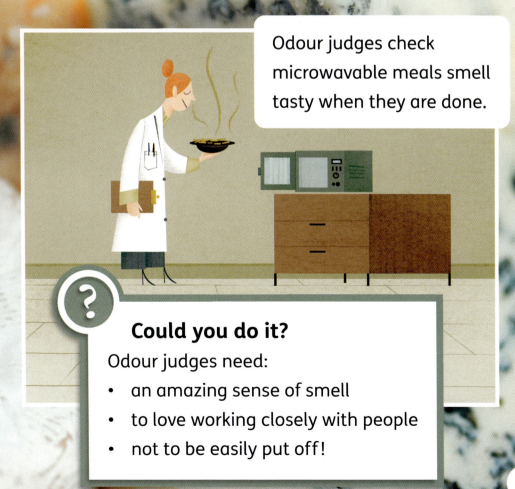

Odour judges check microwavable meals smell tasty when they are done.

Could you do it?
Odour judges need:
- an amazing sense of smell
- to love working closely with people
- not to be easily put off!

Best Pet Food Flavour

This next weird job may ruin your appetite. That's because it involves tasting pet food!

Don't worry, pet food is made with ingredients that are safe for humans. Pet food tasters even say some pet foods taste nice!

Wet cat food is made from meat, vegetables, vitamins, **grains** and gravy.

You should NEVER eat pet food unless it is your job!

A pet food taster's day starts by opening a new can of pet food:
1. First, they smell the food. If it smells bad to a person, it will smell bad to a dog or cat.
2. Next, the taster puts some of the pet food in their mouth. They check the flavour then throw it away – they don't swallow it.
3. Finally, they write a report about the food and how it can be improved.

Could you do it?

Pet food tasters must:
- love trying different flavours
- have a great sense of taste
- be good at writing reports.

Dangerous Divers

Golf is not usually a dangerous sport, but for golf ball divers it can be! They dive into ponds on golf courses to find golf balls that have ended up in the water.

It's dangerous because in some countries, poisonous snakes and even alligators can live in these ponds!

Golfers try to hit their balls over the ponds, but sometimes they miss.

Millions of balls are lost in golf course ponds every year. Golf ball divers find these balls and then sell them back to the golfers.

In the United States, alligators and snakes often attack the golf ball divers. The divers must do a <u>proper</u> check of the pond before they get in.

Divers must be swift to avoid getting hurt when searching for lost balls.

Could you do it?

Golf ball divers must be:
- fast under pressure
- good swimmers
- brave and fearless!

Do you think a <u>proper</u> check of the pond means a quick look around the water's edge, or a careful look at the pond?

The Most Boring Job?

When something is boring, people sometimes joke that it is like watching paint dry. However, watching paint dry is a real job!

Paint watchers check how long it takes for different types of paint to dry. They put the paint on to pieces of cardboard and use a stopwatch to record the drying time.

Paint watchers also look at how paint dries through a **microscope**. They check that the paint dries evenly and the colour lasts well. Paint watchers want to improve how quickly paint dries, how it looks and how long it lasts – which isn't so boring after all!

? Could you do it?

Paint watchers must:
- enjoy science experiments
- pay attention to details
- be very patient!

Bicycle Fishing

People in the Netherlands love to cycle. The country has 17 million people, but over 23 million bikes!

However, in the capital city of Amsterdam, there is a problem. Some people throw their old or broken bikes into the city's many **canals**. This not only pollutes the water, but causes another problem to occur. The bikes scrape and damage boats as they travel along the canals.

Can you name the two problems that occur when people throw their bikes into the canals?

It is the job of bicycle fishers to **haul** bikes from canals. To do this, they use a huge mechanical claw. The claw is fixed to a **barge** that travels up and down Amsterdam's canals. Another barge next to it collects the recovered bikes.

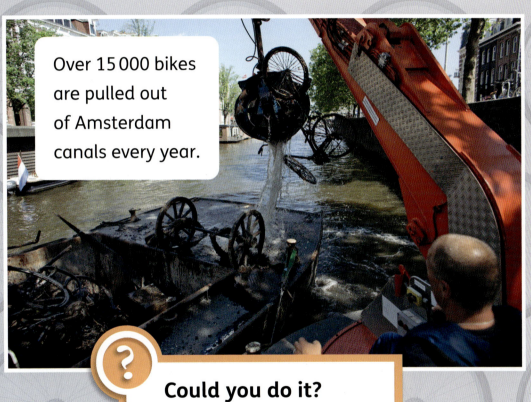

Over 15 000 bikes are pulled out of Amsterdam canals every year.

Could you do it?

Bicycle fishers must:
- like boats and bikes
- be handy with machines
- enjoy working outside.

The World's Weirdest Jobs?

Would you like to do any of the weird jobs in this book when you grow up? Here are a few more to consider.

Passenger pusher

In Japan, trains often get very crowded at rush hour. People are employed to push as many people on to the trains as possible ... but don't try this yourself!

Delivery!

Scuba-diver pizza deliverer

This special diver delivers pizzas to an underwater hotel in Florida, USA. The pizza is stored in a waterproof container.

Teddy bear repair technician

These **technicians** save old teddy bears. They sew eye buttons back on, sew up rips and put the stuffing back in.

Hurricane pilot

These brave pilots fly into hurricanes and record information about the wind, rain and lightning inside the hurricane. They have to be able to control their planes, even in difficult conditions.

Why might it be hard to control a plane in a hurricane?

Glossary

barge: a long boat

canals: rivers that have been made for boats to travel on

deodorant: people put deodorant under their arms to prevent an unpleasant smell

grains: the seeds of plants like corn and wheat

haul: drag or pull

microscope: an instrument with lenses that make tiny details look bigger

odour: a smell

professional: someone who is skilled at the work they do, and is paid for doing it

technicians: people who do practical science or craft work

thrill: feeling of excitement and pleasure

Index

divers..16–17, 22
science..5, 19, 23
senses... 12–13, 14–15
smells..12–13, 15
working outside................ 6–7, 8–9, 10–11, 16–17, 20–21